_____

May the God of hope fill you with
all joy and peace as you trust in him,
so that you may overflow with hope
by the power of the Holy Spirit.

ROMANS 15:13

_____

Margaret Fishback Powers

FOOTPRINTS

AN INTERACTIVE

Journey

THROUGH ONE OF THE MOST

BELOVED POEMS OF

All Time

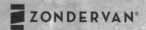

Margaret Fishback Powers

FOOTPRINTS

AN INTERACTIVE
Journey
THROUGH ONE OF THE MOST

BELOVED POEMS OF
All Time

FOOTPRINTS

One night I dreamed a dream.
I was walking along the beach with my Lord.
Across the dark sky flashed scenes from my
    life.
For each scene, I noticed two sets of footprints
    in the sand,
one belonging to me and one to my Lord.
When the last scene of my life shot before me
I looked back at the footprints in the sand
and to my surprise,
I noticed that many times along the path of my
    life
there was only one set of footprints.
I realized that this was at the lowest
and saddest times of my life.
This always bothered me
and I questioned the Lord about my dilemma.

"Lord, you told me when I decided to follow
	You,
You would walk and talk with me all the way.
But I'm aware that during the most
	troublesome
times of my life there is only one set of
	footprints.
I just don't understand why, when I needed
	You most,
You leave me."
He whispered, "My precious child,
I love you and will never leave you
never, ever, during your trials and testings.
When you saw only one set of footprints
it was then that I carried you."

CONTENTS

PREFACE

Every now and then during our devotional time my husband, Paul, and I reread the poem I wrote for him back in 1964. During these times of renewal and prayer, we talk over the events of our lives and share burdens we have for ourselves and others. Very often, we realize that the Great Shepherd has once again reached out and carried us through the day as we spend these introspective moments together.

If the pleasure of sharing these thoughts anew has taught us anything, it is this: that God's word is true. Our Heavenly Father is faithful and will never leave us or forsake us. As we come to Him daily, willing to be shaped and directed, His Word gives guideposts of clear direction. Almost everything we read, see, and experience shows us in some way that, although we do not visibly see God, He is with us. Over centuries of time others have looked back to understand that God's Spirit and presence were there, even when they felt alone.

In our quiet moments of reflection, in the fellowship of others, and in evening dreams, God opens the doors to our hearts. This is what happened when I originally wrote the poem, "Footprints."

After hours of wrestling with the darkness of doubt and despair, I finally surrendered to Him and, in the early morning light of peace, wrote the poem as a result of that spiritual experience.

Listen for the gentle stirring of God's grace in your own mind and soul as you read these verses of encouragement. Each of us is different in our spiritual need, just as each day is different. Reflecting on His Word will help you know Him better.

Spiritual growth is not so much about what we have done, but about the feeling of love for Him we put into everything we do. It is not so much in knowing about God that we grow, but in getting to know Him in a personal, relational way. It is in becoming "a friend of God" as Abraham did that we grow in His grace, talking with Him as our companion along the way, and letting God sift our thoughts and plans through the standards of His Word. May these verses encourage you anew each day as you walk with Him.

—Margaret Fishback Powers

"One night
I dreamed a
dream . . ."

GOD IS
WITH US ...
in our dreams

SOME OF OUR DREAMS CAN HAVE A POWERFUL EFFECT ON US. All of us have, at one time or another, awakened laughing or fretful—and all because of a dream. The Bible tells us about many people who had dreams and visions that were given to them by God.

Some of our dreams are disappointing, but these are "wishful thinking" dreams, things we come up with in our own minds, circumstances or situations that we wish would happen. Only a small portion of these kinds of dreams ever come true. In fact, these dreams can be harmful if we allow them to fill us with false hope.

Still, we should not ignore our dreams. God will sometimes use our dreams to assure us of His promises or to tell us something about Himself. And when God does speak to us in dreams, He will also help us understand them.

Jesus left His disciples with a great promise that is true for us today: "Surely I am with you always, to the very end of the age" (Matthew 28:20).

God's presence with us is a reality. Acts 2:17 also tells us that God will pour His "Spirit on all people." As we dream our dreams with the knowledge that God is with us, we will begin to see things as Christ does and dream dreams inspired by the Holy Spirit that are worth retelling and following.

And afterward,
I will pour out my Spirit on all people.
Your sons and daughters will prophesy,
your old men will dream dreams,
your young men will see visions.
JOEL 2:28

HAS GOD EVER SPOKEN TO YOU IN A DREAM? *If so, what did He show you or how did He reassure you? What are some other ways God speaks to you?*

_____

_____

_____

_____

_____

_____

_____

_____

HAVE YOU EVER BEEN DISAPPOINTED BY A "WISHFUL THINKING" DREAM? *What does God say about putting false hope in them?*

_____

_____

_____

_____

GOD IS WITH US! *How does knowing this impact the way you think and feel about your dreams?*

_____

_____

_____

_____

MY DREAMS

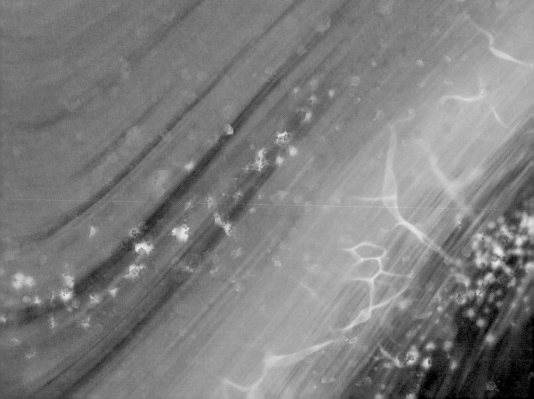

For our light and momentary troubles are achieving for us an eternal glory that far outweighs them all. So we fix our eyes not on what is seen, but on what is unseen, since what is seen is temporary, but what is unseen is eternal.

2 CORINTHIANS 4:17–18

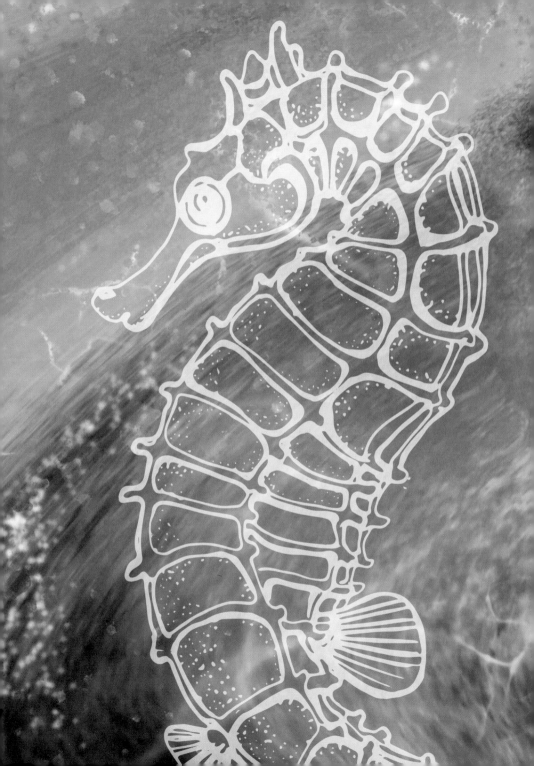

"For I know the plans I have for you," declares the LORD, "plans to prosper you and not to harm you, plans to give you hope and a future. Then you will call on me and come and pray to me, and I will listen to you. You will seek me and find me when you seek me with all your heart."

JEREMIAH 29:11–13

"I was walking
along the beach
with my Lord . . ."

GOD IS WITH US . . .

in our daily walk

13

THE BIBLE TELLS US THAT MAINTAINING A CLOSE WALK WITH GOD IS A COMMAND WE MUST OBEY, NOT MERELY A SUGGESTION WE MAY WANT TO CONSIDER. But what does a walk with God actually entail? How does God want us to live? Deuteronomy 6:5–7 says,

Love the LORD your God with all your heart and with all your soul and with all your strength. These commandments that I give you today are to be upon your hearts. Impress them on your children. Talk about them when you sit at home and when you walk along the road, when you lie down and when you get up.

Many of these things that God asks us to do go against our nature. Yet Nehemiah asks us "Shouldn't you walk in the fear of our God to avoid . . . reproach?" (Nehemiah 5:9). The Bible urges us to walk with the Lord consistently, walking by faith, even when it's difficult.

Health professionals often suggest that people who want to become physically fit should try a consistent program of walking. Sustained walking several times a week will improve your muscle tone and strengthen your heart.

The Bible reassures us that our spiritual lives will also reap benefits when we are consistent in walking with the Lord. Look at the many benefits a walk with God provides include prosperity, blessings, life, and God's protection.

Fanny Crosby once said that the Lord "lovingly guards my footsteps and gives me songs in the night." A joyful heart is the mark of one who has a consistent walk with the Lord, who follows in the footsteps of the Master.

What does the LORD your God ask of you but to fear the LORD your God, to walk in obedience to him, to love him, to serve the LORD your God with all your heart and with all your soul.

DEUTERONOMY 10:12

IN YOUR OWN WORDS, WHAT DOES IT MEAN TO "WALK CLOSELY" WITH GOD? *What things might keep you from your walk with Him?*

_____

_____

_____

_____

_____

_____

_____

READ DEUTERONOMY 6:5–7. *How does your idea of "walking with God" compare with God's commandments in Scripture?*

_____

_____

_____

_____

DESPITE ITS CHALLENGES, WALKING WITH THE LORD HAS POSITIVE RESULTS. *Name some spiritual benefits that can result from consistently walking with God.*

_____

_____

_____

_____

HOW I CAN WALK WITH THE LORD

_____

_____

_____

_____

_____

_____

_____

_____

Although the Lord gives you the bread of adversity and the water of affliction, your teachers will be hidden no more; with your own eyes you will see them. Whether you turn to the right or to the left, your ears will hear a voice behind you, saying, "This is the way; walk in it."

ISAIAH 30:20–21

And this is love: that
we walk in obedience
to his commands. As
you have heard from the
beginning, his command
is that you walk in love.

2 JOHN 6

"Across the dark
sky flashed scenes
from my life."

GOD IS WITH US . . .
in the hard times

We all go through times when life seems to overwhelm us. The Bible reassures us that God's presence is with us to help us, even when we don't realize it. The Book of Psalms is full of reminders that God is a shelter from life's storms, a "refuge and strength, an ever-present help in trouble" (Psalm 46:1) while Ephesians 5:8 reassures us that even though we "were once darkness," we can now "live as children of light."

Moments of darkness in our lives may be caused by the death of a loved one, the loss of a job or a home, or another great tragedy of life. Yet there is a greater darkness than these tragedies: the darkness in the eyes of one who has not felt God's love, grace, and the assurance of His hope. There is hope for all of us. There is light. Jesus Christ, the Son of God, is our hope and light in darkness.

Our dark times may also be times when God wants to teach us something more about ourselves and His love for us. Romans 12:12 advises, "Be joyful in hope, patient in affliction, faithful in prayer." Our faith can be strengthened if we will wait patiently and trust God's heart-desire to make us more like Himself.

Tragedy or testing, dark days or dreary nights, God knows what we are facing. He is in touch with what is happening to us, and He is concerned.

This is the message we have heard from him and declare to you: God is light; in him there is no darkness at all. If we claim to have fellowship with him and yet walk in the darkness, we lie and do not live out the truth. But if we walk in the light, as he is in the light, we have fellowship with one another, and the blood of Jesus, his Son, purifies us from all sin.

1 JOHN 1:5–7

WHEN HAVE YOU BEEN OVERWHELMED BY LIFE? *How did God reveal His presence to you in that time?*

_____

_____

_____

_____

_____

_____

_____

GOD MAY USE OUR DARK TIMES TO DRAW US NEARER TO HIM. *What has God taught you about yourself or His love for you during a dark time?*

_____

_____

_____

_____

READ ISAIAH 43:2. *What does this verse teach you about God's response to our suffering? How can this verse be an encouragement to you in trying times?*

_____

_____

_____

_____

WHAT ENCOURAGES ME

_____

_____

_____

_____

_____

_____

_____

"In my distress I called
to the LORD,
and he answered me.
From deep in the realm of
the dead I called for help,
and you listened to my cry."

JONAH 2:2

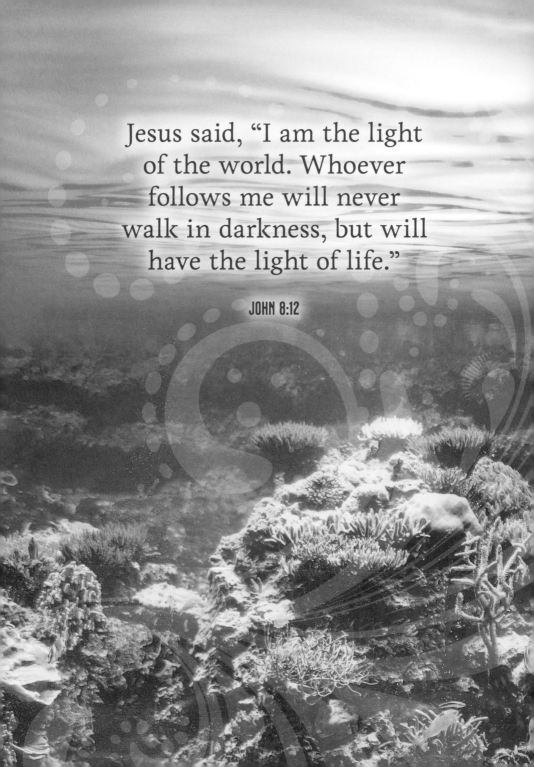

Jesus said, "I am the light of the world. Whoever follows me will never walk in darkness, but will have the light of life."

JOHN 8:12

"For each scene, I noticed two sets of footprints in the sand, one belonging to me and one to my Lord."

GOD IS WITH US . . .
as our companion

I HAVE A FRIEND WHO LOVES TO TAKE LONG WALKS WITH ME. We talk and laugh and enjoy each other's company as we stroll along. The exercise is beneficial, and so is the conversation.

The Lord is a lot like my friend. He enjoys walking with us as our companion on life's pathway. And He brings blessing into our lives when we walk closely with Him.

The awareness of God's presence with us is encouraging and heartwarming. It is as if we were two friends seated beside a rippling brook, enjoying a gentle breeze on a warm spring afternoon. James 4:8 promises, "Come near to God and he will come near to you."

Even when we are surrounded by family and friends, some problems seem to double in size of their own accord. If we toss and turn in the early morning hours thinking about them, they become ten times as large. But remember, the Bible is full of encouragement. Deuteronomy 31:6 tells us to be "strong and courageous. . . . for the LORD your God goes with you; he will never leave you nor forsake you." Though it seems the whole world has gone wrong around us, we are not alone—God is with us!

Wherever we go, we cannot step outside the boundaries of God's love and care. We can have fellowship "with the Father and with his Son, Jesus Christ" wherever we are (1 John 1:3).

All we need to do is trust in God's loving companionship and walk the path He has placed before us.

Blessed are those who have learned to acclaim you,
who walk in the light of your presence, LORD.
PSALM 89:15

WHO IN YOUR LIFE COMES TO MIND WHEN YOU HEAR THE WORD "COMPANION"? *How does your relationship with the Lord compare to that relationship?*

_____

_____

_____

_____

_____

_____

_____

WHAT DOES COMPANIONSHIP WITH GOD LOOK LIKE IN YOUR SPIRITUAL LIFE? *How is it a blessing?*

_____

_____

_____

_____

_____

READ AND REFLECT ON PSALM 139:9–10. *How does the knowledge that God is always with you impact how you respond to painful circumstances or hard times?*

_____

_____

_____

_____

_____

FRIENDS TO RECONNECT WITH

_____

_____

_____

_____

_____

_____

_____

_____

"Though the mountains
be shaken
and the hills be removed,
yet my unfailing love for
you will not be shaken
nor my covenant of
peace be removed,"
says the LORD, who has
compassion on you.

ISAIAH 54:10

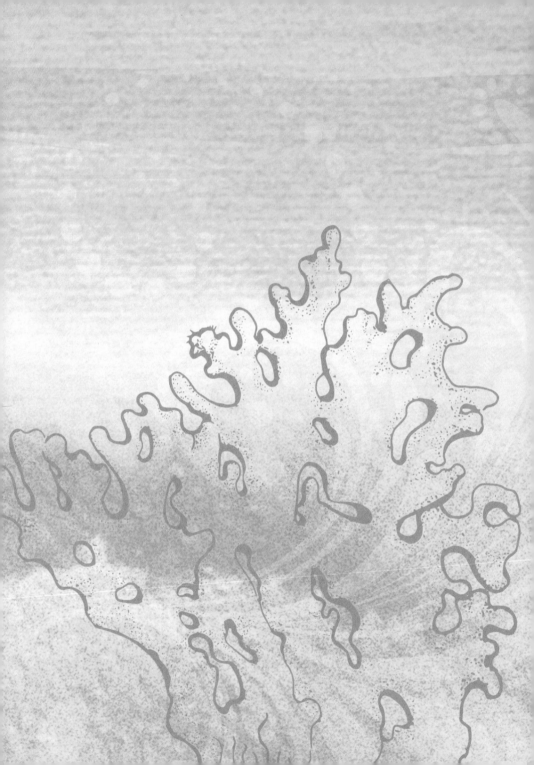

"For
where two or three
gather in my name, there
am I with them."

MATTHEW 18:20

"When the last scene
of my life shot before
me I looked back
at the footprints
in the sand ..."

GOD IS WITH US . . .

in our past, present, and future

WE SAY THAT HINDSIGHT IS ALWAYS 20/20. Looking back is something we often do without considering the consequences. However, looking back is not recommended in the Bible. In Genesis 19, Lot was warned not to look back toward Sodom and Gomorrah. Joshua and his men attacked their enemies in the city of Ai and quickly set the city on fire. When the men of Ai looked back, disaster fell on them.

Even the Lord Jesus reminded His listeners of the perils of looking back: "No one who puts his hand to the plow and looks back is fit for service in the kingdom of God" (Luke 9:62). When we live with an attitude that looks back over our lives with regret and "if only's," we rob ourselves of hope. We rob ourselves of the joy of God's grace.

God never changes. He is the God of grace, hope, and love who offers us a life free of regrets. However, we must move beyond regret to repentance by turning from our sinful ways and embracing God's forgiveness. When we have experienced God's forgiveness, we are new creatures. We can live with a forward-looking hope of glory!

Whenever we do look back over our lives, we must do so with God's perspective, which enables us to trace His hand on our lives and see that He has transformed the bad things of life to good, just as He promised. With God's perspective we will be able to live above regrets and live in God's peace and joy.

Therefore, if anyone is in Christ, the new creation has come: The old has gone, the new is here!

2 CORINTHIANS 5:17

ARE YOU HOLDING ON TO ANYTHING IN YOUR PAST THAT CAUSES YOU REGRET? *What does God say about looking backwards?*

_____

_____

_____

_____

_____

_____

WHAT IS THE DIFFERENCE BETWEEN REGRET AND REPENTANCE? *What does true repentance look like? How can repentance free you from regret?*

_____

_____

_____

_____

_____

SPEND SOME TIME REFLECTING ON YOUR LIFE. *Where can you trace God's hand as He transformed things for your good?*

_____

_____

_____

_____

_____

HOW GOD HAS TRANSFORMED MY LIFE

_____

_____

_____

_____

_____

_____

_____

_____

Surely your goodness
and love will follow me
all the days of my life,
and I will dwell in
the house of the
LORD forever.

PSALM 23:6

Therefore, since we are surrounded by such a great cloud of witnesses, let us throw off everything that hinders and the sin that so easily entangles. And let us run with perseverance the race marked out for us, fixing our eyes on Jesus, the pioneer and perfecter of faith.

HEBREWS 12:1–2

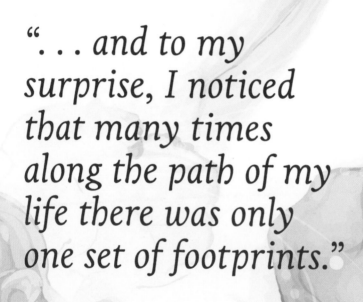

"... and to my surprise, I noticed that many times along the path of my life there was only one set of footprints."

GOD IS WITH US . . .
in our loneliness

TODDLERS OFTEN FACE SEPARATION ANXIETY—A FEELING OF ABANDONMENT WHENEVER THEIR PARENTS LEAVE THE ROOM. Though we may be much older and wiser than little children we still feel the pain of loneliness and isolation. Both Jesus and the psalmist also knew what it was to feel alone, abandoned, and forgotten. Matthew 27:46 describes Jesus crying out loudly, asking His father why He had been forsaken. When we feel alone and abandoned we can take comfort in God's promises to deliver us from our isolation and pain. In fact, we are so lovingly looked after by God that Isaiah tells us we are "engraved on the palms of [His] hands (Isaiah 49:16). Deuteronomy 33:27 promises, "The eternal God is your refuge, and underneath are the everlasting arms."

God is always with us—in our joy and in our pain, in the good times and in the bad times. His steadfast love and faithfulness are promises we can cling to, promises to bring us joy when we face loneliness.

When loneliness overtakes us, we need to remember that we are not alone. God has promised to be with us. He will never forsake us. Lean on His promises, receive His peace, and "put your hope in him" (Psalm 42:11).

Here I am! I stand at the door and knock. If anyone hears my voice and opens the door, I will come in and eat with that person, and they with me.

REVELATION 3:20

READ ISAIAH 41:10. *What is God's promise to you in times of loneliness or isolation? How has God revealed Himself to you in one of these times?*

_____

_____

_____

_____

_____

_____

_____

_____

WHAT PROMISES DOES GOD MAKE TO THOSE WHO ARE LONELY? *What does His faithfulness look like in your life?*

_____

_____

_____

_____

_____

READ ROMANS 8:35-39. *How can this passage reassure you or someone in your life who is struggling with loneliness?*

_____

_____

_____

_____

HOW GOD MEETS ME IN MY LONELINESS

_____

_____

_____

_____

_____

_____

_____

_____

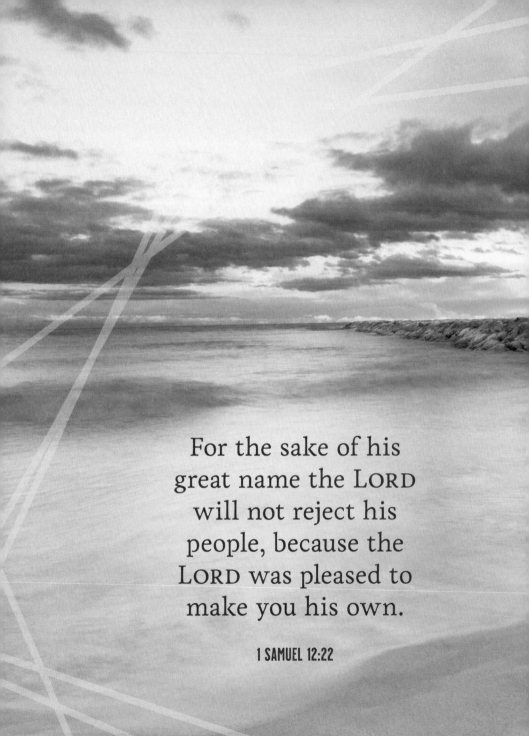

For the sake of his great name the LORD will not reject his people, because the LORD was pleased to make you his own.

1 SAMUEL 12:22

I will not leave you
as orphans; I will
come to you.

JOHN 14:18

"I realized that this was at the lowest and saddest times of my life."

GOD IS
WITH US . . .
in our sorrow

SORROW CAN CAUSE US TO DOUBT GOD'S PLAN. The psalmist cried, "Has his unfailing love vanished forever? Has his promise failed for all time? Has God forgotten to be merciful? Has he in anger withheld his compassion?" (Psalm 77:8–9). Though we may face trouble and difficulties, sadness and pain, God is still in control, and He is always with us.

We must remember to listen closely to God's voice when trouble rages around us. When the agonies of life begin to crush us, God has not moved away from us. Often we have moved away from Him. We need to return to Him in faith and call on Him for His strength.

Jesus experienced sorrow of the deepest kind in the Garden of Gethsemane—the sorrow of impending death. We also experience pain when death takes a loved one, but God reminds us that He is still in control. Death is not the master—God is.

Whether we face death, discouragement, loss, or pain, we can take great comfort in knowing that no sorrow is too deep that God cannot feel it with us. And God wants to help deliver us from it. He wants to bring us His divine comfort.

Though things may seem hopeless, "God, who has called you into fellowship with his Son Jesus Christ our Lord, is faithful" (1 Corinthians 1:9). No trial is so great that God cannot deliver us. No pain is so great that He does not bring us comfort. And no situation is ever without God's presence: "Do not fear, for I am with you; do not be dismayed, for I am your God. I will strengthen you and help you; I will uphold you with my righteous right hand" (Isaiah 41:10).

Yet this I call to mind
and therefore I have hope:
*Because of the L*ORD*'s great love we are not*
consumed,
for his compassions never fail.
They are new every morning;
great is your faithfulness.
LAMENTATIONS 3:21–23

WHAT OR WHOM DO YOU TURN TO WHEN TROUBLE RAGES AROUND YOU? *What is God's desire for you during these times?*

_____

_____

_____

_____

_____

_____

_____

FIRST CORINTHIANS 15:19–22 REMINDS US THAT WE ARE MADE ALIVE IN CHRIST, EVEN IN OUR SORROW. *How has God's Word given you renewed life in a time of grief or pain? How can sharing Scripture with someone who is hurting be an encouragement to them?*

_____

_____

_____

_____

NO SORROW IS TOO DEEP THAT GOD CANNOT FEEL IT WITH YOU. *How does this knowledge change your perspective on God's presence in your pain?*

_____

_____

_____

_____

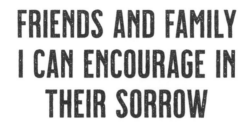

FRIENDS AND FAMILY I CAN ENCOURAGE IN THEIR SORROW

_____

_____

_____

_____

_____

_____

_____

Shout for joy, you heavens;
rejoice, you earth;
burst into song, you
mountains!
For the LORD comforts
his people
and will have compassion
on his afflicted ones.

ISAIAH 49:13

For none of us lives for ourselves alone, and none of us dies for ourselves alone. If we live, we live for the Lord; and if we die, we die for the Lord. So, whether we live or die, we belong to the Lord.

ROMANS 14:7–8

"This always
bothered me . . ."

GOD IS WITH US . . .
in our worry

F RETTING AND A KITCHEN BLENDER HAVE A LOT IN COMMON. With the push of a button the contents of a blender are whirled and swirled until they become a frothy mixture. In our lives, worry gnaws away at us until our lives become a churned jumble. But God doesn't want us to live "blender-ized" lives.

Fretting easily leads to worry; worry casts a big shadow over small problems—a shadow that should never cross our lives.

When the outlook is not good, we should not fret. We need a change of perspective to realize that God sees tomorrow more clearly than we see yesterday. The future is completely in His hands!

Don't fret! Cheer up! Neither the sun, nor the Son, has gone out of business. He is with us. A new day will dawn and the Lord will bring Himself to the center of our problems.

Remember, worry will only tie us in knots. Prayer is the only way to cut short our fretting—to cut those knots of worry and care and grant us God's peace instead.

Do not be anxious about anything, but in every situation, by prayer and petition, with thanksgiving, present your requests to God. And the peace of God, which transcends all understanding, will guard your hearts and your minds in Christ Jesus.

PHILIPPIANS 4:6–7

HOW CAN FRETTING LEAD TO WORRY? *What does Jesus say about the consequences of worrying in Matthew 6:27–30?*

_____

_____

_____

_____

_____

_____

_____

CONSIDER THE THINGS YOU WORRY ABOUT. *What happens to your worry when you change your perspective and realize that God holds your tomorrow in His hands?*

_____

_____

_____

_____

_____

READ JEREMIAH 17:7-8. *What does it look like in your life to be rooted by your trust in the Lord? How can these roots support you when worry threatens to overwhelm you?*

_____

_____

_____

_____

_____

WORRIES I'M GIVING TO THE LORD

_____

_____

_____

_____

_____

_____

_____

_____

"But blessed is the one
who trusts in the LORD,
whose confidence is in him.
They will be like a tree
planted by the water
that sends out its roots
by the stream.
It does not fear when
heat comes;
its leaves are always green.
It has no worries in
a year of drought
and never fails to bear fruit."

JEREMIAH 17:7–8

Then Jesus said to his disciples: "Therefore I tell you, do not worry about your life, what you will eat; or about your body, what you will wear. For life is more than food, and the body more than clothes."

LUKE 12:22–23

". . . and I questioned the Lord about my dilemma."

GOD IS WITH US . . .
when we need direction

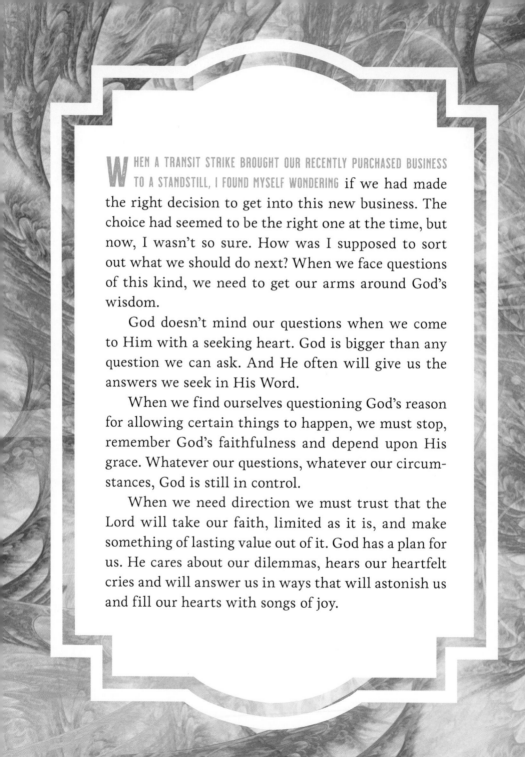

WHEN A TRANSIT STRIKE BROUGHT OUR RECENTLY PURCHASED BUSINESS TO A STANDSTILL, I FOUND MYSELF WONDERING if we had made the right decision to get into this new business. The choice had seemed to be the right one at the time, but now, I wasn't so sure. How was I supposed to sort out what we should do next? When we face questions of this kind, we need to get our arms around God's wisdom.

God doesn't mind our questions when we come to Him with a seeking heart. God is bigger than any question we can ask. And He often will give us the answers we seek in His Word.

When we find ourselves questioning God's reason for allowing certain things to happen, we must stop, remember God's faithfulness and depend upon His grace. Whatever our questions, whatever our circumstances, God is still in control.

When we need direction we must trust that the Lord will take our faith, limited as it is, and make something of lasting value out of it. God has a plan for us. He cares about our dilemmas, hears our heartfelt cries and will answer us in ways that will astonish us and fill our hearts with songs of joy.

"Let us acknowledge the LORD;
let us press on to acknowledge him.
As surely as the sun rises,
he will appear;
he will come to us like the winter rains,
like the spring rains that water the earth."
HOSEA 6:3

READ GOD'S ENCOURAGEMENT IN ISAIAH 30:21. *Think of times in your life when you felt like God helped you move in a different direction. How did taking another path make you feel?*

_____

_____

_____

_____

_____

_____

_____

HAVE YOU EVER BEEN SO LOST YOU HAD TO ASK FOR DIRECTIONS? *Did you feel embarrassed to need assistance, or were you uplifted that someone else knew the way? What does this look like in our faith walk?*

_____

_____

_____

_____

LIFE CAN GET DIFFICULT. *What are some ways that help you find your way back to God's faithfulness and rely on His grace?*

_____

_____

_____

_____

AREAS WHERE I NEED
THE LORD'S DIRECTION

_____

_____

_____

_____

_____

_____

_____

_____

For this command
is a lamp,
this teaching is a light,
and correction and
instruction
are the way to life.

PROVERBS 6:23

The LORD will guide
you always;
he will satisfy your needs
in a sun-scorched land
and will strengthen
your frame.
You will be like a well-
watered garden,
like a spring whose
waters never fail.

ISAIAH 58:11

"Lord, You told me when I decided to follow You . . ."

GOD IS WITH US . . .
in our decisions

IT SEEMS THAT SOMETIMES ALL WE DO IS MAKE DECISIONS. Purchases at the grocery store are easy, but life-changing decisions are more difficult. How can God help us? The Book of Proverbs generously shows us how, telling us that God will "guide [us] in the way of wisdom and lead [us] along straight paths" (4:11), and that if we "trust in the LORD with all [our] heart . . . he will make [our] paths straight (3:5, 6).

The decisions we need to make may be simple or complex, but they should always be predicated on our decision to follow the Lord.

Following the Lord means we must live our lives the way He wants us to, following His commands, yielded to His control. Romans 12:1–2 provides a blueprint to help us make godly decisions, which serve as forms of worship: "Offer your bodies as a living sacrifice, holy and pleasing to God—this is your true and proper worship. Do not conform to the pattern of this world, but be transformed by the renewing of your mind." First Timothy 6:11–12 also presents a clear path to a faith journey guided by the light of God's will: "Pursue righteousness, godliness, faith, love, endurance and gentleness. Fight the good fight of the faith."

We all need God's divine power from day to day to follow in His footsteps—to learn the eternal, upside-down, inside-out values of God's kingdom so that we may make decisions based on His character and ultimately share in His glory.

For the grace of God has appeared that offers salvation to all people. It teaches us to say "No" to ungodliness and worldly passions, and to live self-controlled, upright and godly lives in this present age.

TITUS 2:11-12

WHAT DOES JOSHUA 22:5 IMPLORE US TO DO? *How does our decision-making help us love and serve God more faithfully?*

_____

_____

_____

_____

_____

_____

_____

SOME DECISIONS ARE EASY WHILE OTHERS ARE COMPLICATED AND TIME-CONSUMING.
Reflect on the ways God supports us even as we make the simplest of decisions. Are difficult decisions more "worthy" in God's eyes? Why or why not?

_____

_____

_____

_____

_____

THINK OF A TIME WHEN YOU MADE A WRONG DECISION. *How did God comfort you during this time of self-doubt? What did God's grace look like during this time?*

_____

_____

_____

_____

_____

DECISIONS I CAN ENTRUST TO GOD

_____

_____

_____

_____

_____

_____

_____

_____

"Keep the commandment and the law that Moses the servant of the LORD gave you: to love the LORD your God, to walk in obedience to him, to keep his commands, to hold fast to him and to serve him with all your heart and with all your soul."

JOSHUA 22:5

If anyone speaks, they should do so as one who speaks the very words of God. If anyone serves, they should do so with the strength God provides, so that in all things God may be praised through Jesus Christ.

1 PETER 4:11

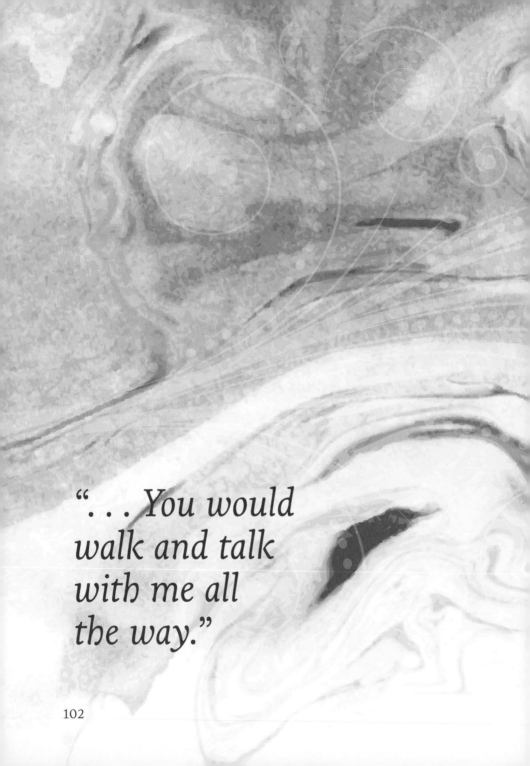

"... *You would walk and talk with me all the way.*"

GOD IS WITH US

as our guide

I SAW TWO CHILDREN WALKING TOGETHER TODAY, happily exchanging words and glances, laughing aloud at shared jokes. They didn't worry about the cracks in the sidewalk or the bumps in the road, but rather skipped along over them. God wants our walk with Him to be just like that—enjoying His company, sharing together, and crossing the rough places on our journey home without the slightest care.

Many times along our life-walk the path becomes obscure. We need someone to help show us the way. That someone is God. Isaiah 2:3 assures us that "He will teach us his ways, so that we may walk in his paths." Isaiah 58:11 shows that God's eternal guidance will make us "like a well-watered garden, like a spring whose waters never fail." What a beautiful image from which we can find comfort and confidence!

God's Word becomes our road map for our daily walk with the Savior. His Word reminds us of His power, His provision, and His sovereignty. Jeremiah 29:11 reveals that the Lord has wonderful plans for us, "plans to prosper [us] and not to harm [us], plans to give [us] hope and a future.

His Word reminds us of His love, a love that is "new every morning" (Lamentations 3:23), just like the rising sun.

Let's enjoy the time with God as He walks and talks with us each day, wherever we are, for "this God is our God for ever and ever; he will be our guide even to the end" (Psalm 48:14).

> Whoever claims to live in him must live
> as Jesus did.
>
> **1 JOHN 2:6**

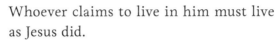 *Using a concordance or online search tool, look up "laughter" in the Bible. What do these verses tell us about how important joy is in God's guidance?*

_____

_____

_____

_____

_____

_____

_____

PSALM 48:14 TELLS US GOD "WILL BE OUR GUIDE EVEN TO THE END." *What does it look like when you trust God as your guide through life?*

_____

_____

_____

_____

_____

THE WELL-KNOWN WORDS OF PSALM 119 TELL US SCRIPTURE IS "A LAMP TO [OUR] FEET AND A LIGHT FOR [OUR] PATH." *Reflect on ways God uses the Bible to illuminate our journey. In what other ways has God guided you?*

_____

_____

_____

_____

_____

TIMES THAT I FELT GOD'S GUIDANCE

_____

_____

_____

_____

_____

_____

_____

_____

_____

"Remember, LORD,
how I have walked
before you faithfully
and with wholehearted
devotion and have
done what is good
in your eyes."

2 KINGS 20:3

If any of you
lacks wisdom, you should ask
God, who gives generously
to all without finding fault,
and it will be given to you.

JAMES 1:5

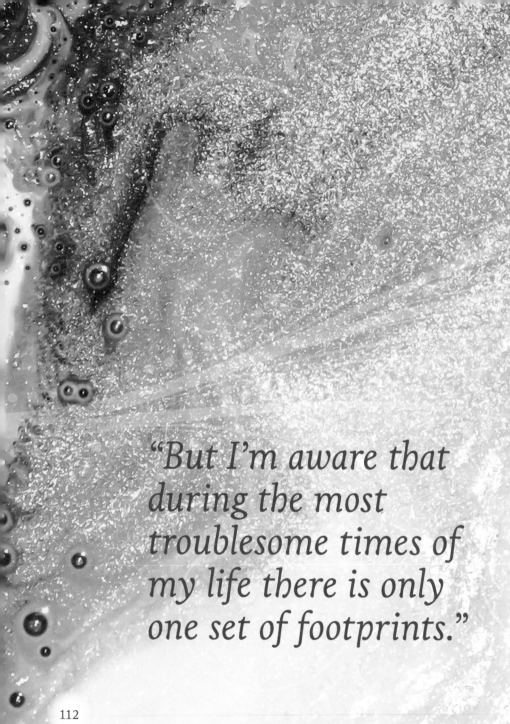

"But I'm aware that during the most troublesome times of my life there is only one set of footprints."

GOD IS WITH US . . .
in our difficulties

RUTS AND POTHOLES. SHADOWS AND DEEP DARKNESS. THE JOURNEY OF LIFE CAN SOMETIMES BE VERY TROUBLING. We stumble and have difficulty following in God's footsteps. We are fearful of the unknown. But God's Word reminds us to trust, to believe, to hope.

Throughout the Psalms, we are repeatedly emboldened to remain strong as we encounter obstacles in our path: "Be strong and take heart, all you who hope in the LORD (Psalm 31:24). The psalmist reasons confidently in Psalm 56:3–4, "When I am afraid, I will trust in you. In God, whose word I praise, in God I trust; I will not be afraid. What can mortal man do to me?" And then he declares in Psalm 71:5, "You have been my hope, O Sovereign LORD, my confidence since my youth.

Granted, we all go through troubling times, but we must never doubt God's presence with us. Jesus says in Matthew 28:20, "Surely I am with you always, to the very end of the age."

God will never let us down. He promises us His strength, His peace, His comfort and His presence. All we need to do is depend on Him, for we can never break God's promises by leaning on them. They are steadfast and everlasting.

Those things we consider difficulties are often God's opportunities for our greater blessing. We must trust, believe, hope and continue to walk the path He has laid before us.

> Who shall separate us from the love of Christ? Shall trouble or hardship or persecution or famine or nakedness or danger or sword? . . . No, in all these things we are more than conquerors through him who loved us.
>
> ROMANS 8:35, 37

READ NAHUM 1:7. *Think of times you had to rely on God to shelter you from danger. How did you respond each time?*

_____

_____

_____

_____

_____

_____

_____

IMAGINE YOUR FAITH JOURNEY AS A SMOOTH, PERFECTLY PAVED ROAD. *That sounds ideal, but is it true to real life? How does God use the ruts and potholes of our lives to love, guide, and comfort us?*

_____

_____

_____

_____

HOW DOES GOD USE THE DIFFICULT TIMES IN LIFE AS OPPORTUNITIES FOR SOMETHING GREATER? *How have you seen God's blessing in your own life during a challenging time?*

_____

_____

_____

_____

DIFFICULTIES I AM STRUGGLING WITH RIGHT NOW

_____

_____

_____

_____

_____

_____

_____

May our Lord Jesus Christ himself and God our Father, who loved us and by his grace gave us eternal encouragement and good hope, encourage your hearts and strengthen you in every good deed and word.

2 THESSALONIANS 2:16–17

The LORD is a refuge
for the oppressed,
a stronghold in times
of trouble.
Those who know your
name trust in you,
for you, LORD, have never
forsaken those who seek you.

PSALM 9:9-10

"I just don't understand why, when I needed You the most, You leave me."

GOD IS WITH US . . .
in our confusion

MANY THINGS IN LIFE CANNOT BE EXPLAINED. The death of an infant, the loss of a job, the rebellion of a child, the desertion by a loved one, or any number of circumstances beyond our control often cause us to wonder, *Why did this have to happen?* God can help us with those "Why?" questions.

Even David, who was known as "a man after [God's] own heart" (1 Samuel 13:14), found himself confused and questioning the Lord:

> "Has his unfailing love vanished forever?
> Has his promise failed for all time?
> Has God forgotten to be merciful?
> Has he in anger withheld his compassion?"
>
> PSALM 77:8–9

When faced with bewildering circumstances, we are tempted to ask "Why?" But perhaps a better question to ask is "What? What do You have in mind now, Lord?"

Though it may sometimes seem that things are out of control, we can take comfort in God's enduring promises and constant presence. Put away all doubts. Cast out all confusion. Stand firm in the work of the Lord and find a renewed faith following in His footsteps. As the psalmist pronounces in Psalm 28:7,

> The LORD is my strength and my shield;
> my heart trusts in him, and I am helped.
> My heart leaps for joy and I will give thanks to him.

> "Call to me and I will answer you and tell you great and unsearchable things you do not know."
>
> JEREMIAH 33:3

SOMETIMES NOT HAVING ALL THE ANSWERS IN TIMES OF DESPAIR OR GRIEF FEELS LIKE CONFUSION. *In addition to God, whom do you depend on to help you through your feelings of confusion? List them here and write a brief prayer of gratitude for having them in your life.*

_____

_____

_____

_____

_____

_____

_____

"BEWILDER" CAN MEAN "TO LOSE ONE'S BEARINGS." *Think of times when you felt lost or uncertain. How did God intervene and help you regain peace of mind?*

_____

_____

_____

_____

_____

LIFE IS FULL OF UNEXPLAINABLE CIRCUMSTANCES. *How would you explain the unexplainable to a child or someone completely baffled by their circumstances? Describe the ways God helps us cope with uncertainty.*

_____

_____

_____

_____

_____

HOW GOD HAS GIVEN ME CLARITY IN MY LIFE

_____

_____

_____

_____

_____

_____

_____

_____

Let us hold unswervingly to the hope we profess, for he who promised is faithful.

HEBREWS 10:23

There is a time for everything,
and a season for every
activity under the heavens:
. . . . a time to weep
and a time to laugh,
a time to mourn and
a time to dance.

ECCLESIASTES 3:1, 4–5

"He whispered,
'My precious
child . . .'"

GOD IS WITH US . . .

as our loving father

133

THE CREATOR OF THE UNIVERSE CALLS US HIS CHILDREN—WHAT A BLESSING! What a privilege! What a responsibility! Both Testaments explore in depth the most important parent/child relationship we could ever encounter. Proverbs 3:12 tells us "the LORD disciplines those he loves, as a father the son he delights in." We are reminded of God's loving parental promise in 2 Corinthians 6:18: "I will be a Father to you, and you will be my sons and daughters." The psalmist shows how well David understood the relationship: "You are my Father, my God, the Rock my Savior" (Psalm 89:26).

As children of God we can trust that our Father will provide for us. Jesus was very clear on this point: "Your Father knows what you need before you ask him" (Matthew 6:8). Later, when Jesus taught His disciples how to pray what we now call the Lord's Prayer, He offered another profound illustration of our relationship with God:

> "Which of you fathers, if your son asks for a fish, will give him a snake instead? Or if he asks for an egg, will give him a scorpion? If you then, though you are evil, know how to give good gifts to your children, how much more will your Father in heaven give the Holy Spirit to those who ask him!"
>
> LUKE 11:11-13

Because we are God's children, our Father knows us by name and bestows on us certain rights, privileges, and responsibilities. Our loving Father cares for us as a shepherd cares for his sheep. And we, His children, need to listen carefully to His voice and obey. Again, Jesus was clear: "My sheep listen to my voice; I know them, and they follow me" (John 10:27)..

Before I was born the LORD called me;
from my mother's womb he has spoken
my name.

ISAIAH 49:1

YOU ARE A CHILD OF THE CREATOR! *How does knowing and embracing that make you feel? What are some ways you can encourage others by reminding them of this truth?*

_____

_____

_____

_____

_____

_____

_____

_____

OUR EARTHLY FATHERS CAN BE FAR FROM PERFECT. *What are some ways we humans project our relationship with our own fathers on our relationship with God? Is that good or bad? Why or why not?*

_____

_____

_____

_____

_____

JESUS OFTEN DISCUSSED GOD AND HUMANITY USING THE METAPHOR OF A SHEPHERD TENDING HIS SHEEP. *What are some specific examples from your own life when God looked after you as a shepherd after his sheep?*

_____

_____

_____

_____

_____

WAYS THAT THE LORD IS MY FATHER

_____

_____

_____

_____

_____

_____

_____

_____

For to us a child is born,
to us a son is given,
and the government will
be on his shoulders.
And he will be called
Wonderful Counselor,
Mighty God,
Everlasting Father,
Prince of Peace.

ISAIAH 9:6

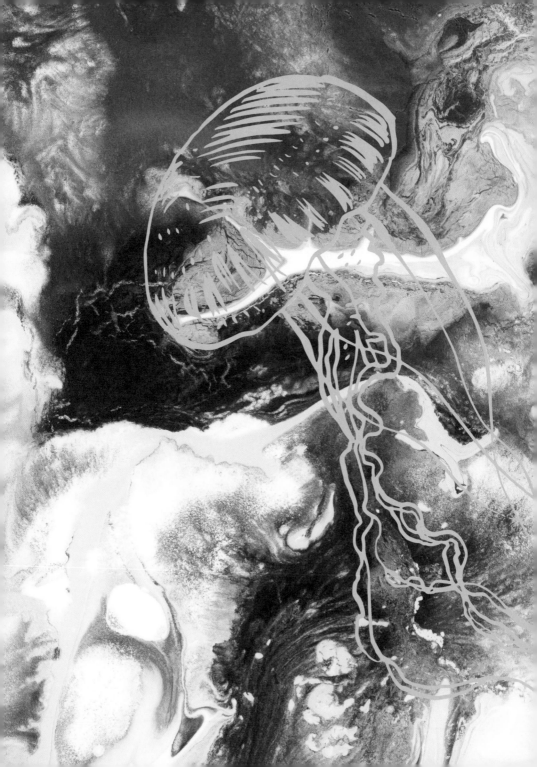

See what great
love the Father has
lavished on us, that
we should be called
children of God! And
that is what we are!

1 JOHN 3:1

". . . I love you and will never leave you never, ever, during your trials and testings."

GOD IS WITH US . . .
always!

WE OFTEN MAKE PROMISES WE CAN'T KEEP. God isn't like that. God is faithful and trustworthy. When God promised "Never will I leave you; never will I forsake you" (Hebrews 13:5), He meant just what He said. He's not going anywhere!

Joshua 1:5 tells us that God's love for us is eternal: "No one will be able to stand against you all the days of your life. As I was with Moses, so I will be with you." In his letter to the Romans, Paul argues that God's love God goes far beyond any limited, human understanding of love:

> For I am convinced that neither death nor life, neither angels nor demons, neither the present nor the future, nor any powers, neither height nor depth, nor anything else in all creation, will be able to separate us from the love of God that is in Christ Jesus our Lord.
>
> ROMANS 8:38–39

When it seems that life is whirling out of control, we can take comfort in God's sovereignty and power. He has everything under control. And He will work His will in every circumstance. As Proverbs 19:21 says, "Many are the plans in a person's heart, but it is the LORD's purpose that prevails." You can rest in the knowledge that God is powerful enough and loving enough to shelter you in His loving arms: "Cast all your anxiety on him because he cares for you" (1 Peter 5:7).

Whenever we hit rock-bottom, we cn be assured of God's love and care. His encouragement breathes new possibilities into impossible circumstances.

The LORD will keep you from all harm—
he will watch over your life;
the LORD will watch over your coming and
going
both now and forevermore.

PSALM 121:7–8

"FOREVERMORE" IS A LONG TIME. *Imagine if God had promised He would be with us by appointment only or only on Tuesdays and Thursdays! What is the significance of God's promise in Hebrews 13:5?*

_____

_____

_____

_____

_____

_____

_____

READ ROMANS 8:38-39 AGAIN. *It reassures us that nothing can separate us from God's love. What are some images that come to mind when you reflect on this unbreakable bond?*

_____

_____

_____

_____

_____

GOD NEVER BREAKS HIS PROMISES, BUT NO HUMAN IS PERFECT. *Think of a time when you or someone you loved broke a promise. How did that make you feel? How did God help you heal from that pain?*

_____

_____

_____

_____

_____

PROMISES GOD HAS MADE TO ME

_____

_____

_____

_____

_____

_____

_____

_____

So do not fear, for I
am with you;
do not be dismayed,
for I am your God.
I will strengthen you
and help you;
I will uphold you with my
righteous right hand.

ISAIAH 41:10

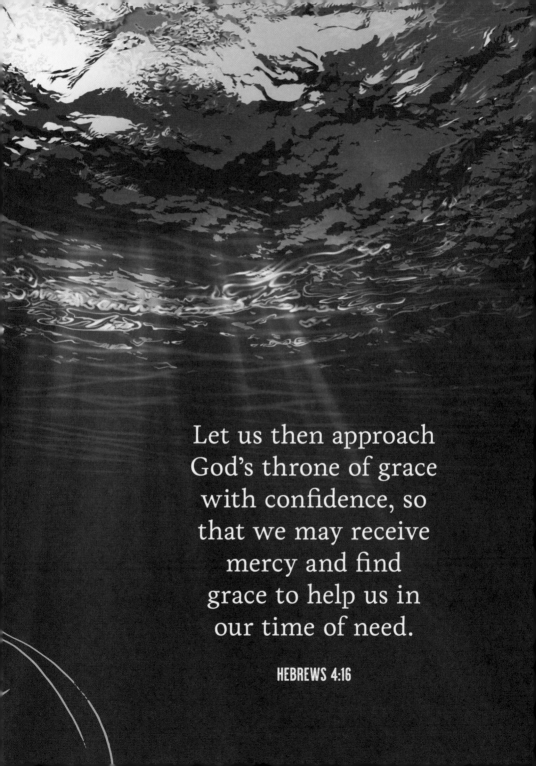

Let us then approach God's throne of grace with confidence, so that we may receive mercy and find grace to help us in our time of need.

HEBREWS 4:16

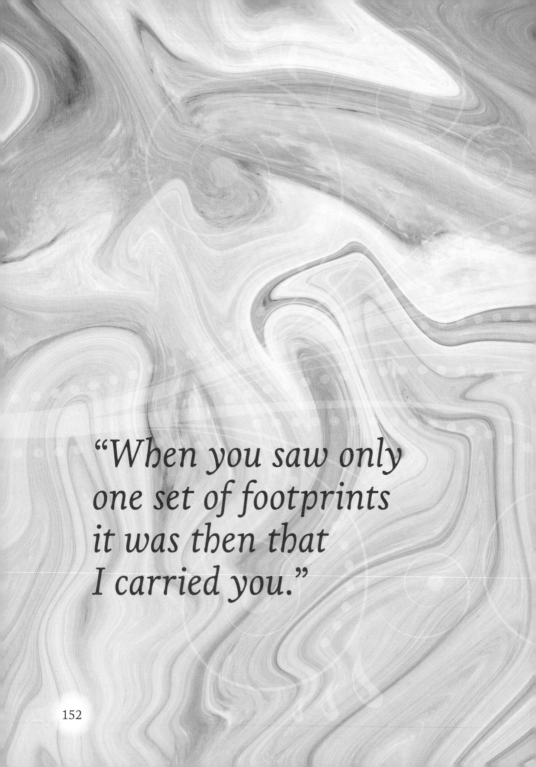

"When you saw only
one set of footprints
it was then that
I carried you."

GOD IS WITH US . . .
as our strong provider

OUR PROBLEMS MAY SEEM OVERWHELMING, BUT GOD'S POWER IS STRONGER THAN ANY OBSTACLE WE MAY FACE. Throughout Scripture God's power is meant not only to comfort us when our troubles distract us but also to give us confidence as we travel on our faith journey. First Chronicles reveals the far-reaching effects of God's hand:

> *You are the ruler of all things.*
> > *In your hands are strength and power*
> > *to exalt and give strength to all.*
> *Now, our God, we give you thanks,*
> > *and praise your glorious name.*
> > 1 CHRONICLES 29:12–13

We hear the strength of God's voice in Jeremiah: "I am the LORD, the God of all mankind. Is anything too hard for me?" (Jeremiah 32:27). In the New Testament, we realize God's love includes wanting us to succeed: "Not that we are competent in ourselves to claim anything for ourselves, but our competence comes from God (2 Corinthians 3:5). Jesus assured us that our future in God was full of hope and joy: "With God all things are possible" (Matthew 19:26). And Paul reiterated this hope: "I can do all this through him who gives me strength" (Philippians 4:13).

Since God is our strong Provider, we can be assured that He will provide for our every need. We can rest in Jesus's comforting promise: "Come to me, all you who are weary and burdened, and I will give you rest" (Matthew 11:28).

Our God is strong enough to carry us, but also gentle enough to enfold us in His loving embrace.

God will command his angels concerning you
to guard you in all your ways;
they will lift you up in their hands,
so that you will not strike your foot
against a stone.
PSALM 91:11-12

"OMNIPOTENT" IS A WORD OFTEN USED TO DESCRIBE GOD. *It means "all-powerful."*
How have you seen God's power working in your life?

_____

_____

_____

_____

_____

_____

_____

SECOND CORINTHIANS 3:5 TELLS US "OUR COMPETENCE COMES FROM GOD." *Think of a time when you felt overwhelmed or incompetent. What are some ways that God helps us combat those feelings of inadequacy and regain our confidence and closeness to Him?*

_____

_____

_____

_____

_____

READ ISAIAH 40:11. *This verse portrays God's strength as well as His gentleness. What are some specific ways God has been both powerful and gentle with you?*

_____

_____

_____

_____

_____

TIMES THAT GOD CARRIED ME

_____

_____

_____

_____

_____

_____

_____

_____

"Whoever drinks the water I give them will never thirst. Indeed, the water I give them will become in them a spring of water welling up to eternal life.

JOHN 4:14

I will strengthen
them in the LORD
and in his name they
will live securely,"
declares the LORD.

ZECHARIAH 10:12

About the Author

Margaret Fishback Powers is the author of the world-famous "Footprints" poem. When she wrote the poem in 1964, she was a young woman searching for direction at a crossroads in her life. She has traveled the world as an evangelist with her husband, Paul, for more than fifty years.